WORK
THE MEANING OF YOUR LIFE

A CHRISTIAN PERSPECTIVE

WORK

THE MEANING OF YOUR LIFE

A CHRISTIAN PERSPECTIVE

Second Edition

LESTER DEKOSTER

Foreword by Stephen J. Grabill

Afterword by The Oikonomia Network

Christian's LIBRARY PRESS

GRAND RAPIDS · MICHIGAN

Work: The Meaning of Your Life
A Christian Perspective

© 1982 by Lester DeKoster (1916–2009)

First edition published 1982. Second edition 2010.

Cover image: Balogh, Balage
Nehemiah Rebuilding Jerusalem's Walls
Source: © Balage Balogh / Art Resource, NY

ISBN 10: 1-880595-72-9
ISBN 13: 978-1-880595-72-5

Library of Congress Cataloging-in-Publication Data

DeKoster, Lester (1916–2009)
      Work: The Meaning of Your Life / DeKoster, Lester
      A Christian Perspective

CHRISTIAN'S LIBRARY PRESS
   *An imprint of the Acton Institute
   for the Study of Religion & Liberty*

161 Ottawa Avenue, NW, Suite 301
Grand Rapids, Michigan 49503
Phone: 616.454.3080
Fax: 616.454.9454
www.clpress.com

Cover design by Peter Ho
Interior composition by Judy Schafer and Jan M. Ortiz

Printed in the United States of America

To Buzz

Lay a blanket of seeds upon a field ...
And behold ... a harvest!
Lay a blanket of work upon the world ...
And behold ... a civilization!

CONTENTS

FOREWORD

The staying power of Lester DeKoster's little booklet is due to his foresight in seeing work as a manifestation of whole-life discipleship. You can find countless authors writing about the ills of the workplace, better ways to manage time and resources, daily planning and organizational practices, the moral character of the worker, workplace ethics, and so on, but few ever take up the theological significance of work itself. And even fewer still, slow down long enough to reflect on the spirituality *and* economics of work from a macro-level perspective. Not so with Lester DeKoster; he probes these topics with his characteristic wit, keen intellect, and rhetorical acumen. The result is a book with mass appeal and convicting power that is still insightful twenty-eight years after its original publication.

Why is this the case? It is because he stays focused on a perennial question, "Does work give meaning to life?" His resounding affirmation uncovers three essential insights that make this book a must read for anyone who has ever wondered whether work is really a divine institution and not merely a necessary evil.

The first insight is that work, indeed, gives meaning to life because it is the form in which we make ourselves useful to others, and thus to God. God accomplishes his purposes in the world by equipping us with talents, skills, and abilities that he expects us to use in service to others.

The second insight, building on the collective wisdom of the free-market tradition, is that our work shares in weaving civilization, which is the form in which others make themselves useful to us, by providing us with the tools for doing our work well. This is reminiscent of Adam Smith's famous remark about the brewer, the butcher, and the baker in the *Wealth of Nations* (Bk. III, chap. 1).

And, finally, work sculpts the kind of self we are becoming through the choices we make in the handling of our talents on the job. DeKoster writes: "The chisel we use to sculpt our selves is choice. It's not a chisel of our own making: it's a tool we can't avoid using.... Selves are formed into sheep or goat by the 'god' we serve in the choices we make in all of life."

Evangelicals have always had an implicit sense that work is good because it carries out the cultural mandate, but rarely, if ever, have they thought of work as one of the core elements of discipleship and spiritual formation. In fact, one of the most pressing needs among evangelicals today is to revive a commitment to whole-life discipleship. Christianity is about so much more than what happens for an hour or two on Sunday morning; it's a way of life and it affects every area of our lives, including our working life.

With the passing of Lester DeKoster in 2009, the Acton Institute assumed the leadership of Christian's Library Press, the imprint that Lester DeKoster and Gerard Berghoef founded in 1979. Given the Acton Institute's interest in the relationship between work, stewardship, and economics—in other words, biblical *oikonomia*—it makes sense for us to issue a second edition of *Work: The Meaning of Your Life*, in various formats fit for a new generation. The second edition features a new Foreword and Afterword, the latter of which is an excerpt of The Oikonomia Network's longer Manifesto ("Whatever You Do: Why Discipleship Is Withering—and What We Can Do About It"). This new edition also includes a light edit and update of the text, as well as the alteration of biblical citations from the Revised Standard Version in the first edition to the New International Version of Scripture now in the second edition.

My hope is simple: Read and understand, and pray that God will open the windows of heaven to bring about a revolution in seminary education and church life in our day, one that will finally mobilize the whole people of God to grasp the full implication of Colossians 3:23–24: "Whatever you do, work at it with all your heart, as working for the Lord, not for men, since you know that you will receive an inheritance from the Lord as a reward. It is the Lord Christ you are serving."

—Stephen J. Grabill, Ph.D.
Senior Research Scholar in Theology
Acton Institute

General Editor
NIV Stewardship Study Bible

PREFACE

Work gets the largest single block of our lives.

Yet we tend to look for meaningful living anywhere but on the job.

We work daily for the paycheck that tries to keep necessity at bay and provides us enough leisure besides to pursue what seems to give meaning to our existence.

We don't quite work just to eat nor eat just to work—at least we don't want to. However, it often comes down near to that, and time on the job is for too many of us time at the rat race—with the rats winning.

Sometimes we pause to wonder: Is this, then, what life amounts to—a wilderness of work broken with oases of meaning furnished by our families, the church, politics, community affairs, plus hobbies and spectator sports thrown in to give some zest to leisure?

Is this "it"?

I used to think so. Do you now?

Not that most of us expect to make some big splash in the news—those who do are soon eclipsed by new faces on our TV screens anyhow. Who was who, just yesterday? We do crave sensing, somehow, that we count for more than we can control with our income or do with our spare time. Our hearts whisper that life *must* have some meaning besides the poet's "getting and spending...."

One day two things dawned on me: (1) If life is to have meaning, I would have to find it, not hope to create it for myself. (2) Living must get its meaning, first of all, on the job, because that's the drain down in which the best hours of every week dribble away.

At first, these options seemed fanciful: Life's meaning on the job? Not because I put it there, but because *work* endows living with significance? Kidding somebody?

No kidding at all. That's the way it is. Come along and see for yourself!

Looking back, I noticed that I had made this little adventure in perception without going anywhere in particular—leading me also to think that the most important journeys we can take are those that shift our outlook, right at home. Not too far to travel!

I write this booklet so that you can share, if you want to, the same discovery: It *is* your daily work, whatever your job, that does give meaning to your life, not because you will now decide to put meaning there but because God has already done so.

And what, by the way, is meant here by "meaning"?

Meaning is the answer to the "what fors" of life. Why work? Why play? Why do anything at all? What is it all about? Such queries probe for meaning, no less in the lives of the jet set than in those of the frustrated and poor. Meaning gets rounded out, of course, beyond the job—in our families, our religious and community activities, our friends, and on vacations, dabbling with our hobbies, and so forth. However, working takes the core of the week for most of us, and if the job drains life of meaning then all else is shadowed too—how heavy hangs next Monday morning over the whole weekend for the many who loathe their jobs.

If work can give a central core of meaning to living, then all other meanings cluster around this one.

Therefore, a right view of work becomes the key to a satisfying life, as it now looks to me. And whenever, and wherever, I see people working—at any kind of work, such as head or hand, blue-collar or white-collar, trade or profession—I want to shout out the good news: *This* gives meaning to your life! Right here! Right now!

Come and see.

1

WHAT IS WORK?

Work Is the Form in Which We Make Ourselves Useful to Others

The Secret

This is really the open secret of all that follows: *Work is the form in which we make ourselves useful to others.*

I'm not saying that's the way I always looked at my jobs. I'm not saying that's how you should look at yours now. But that is, I am convinced, the essence of working: making ourselves useful to others.

That is why work gives meaning to life.

Work means here, remember, everybody's job, from that paid in executive salaries and bonuses to that unpaid in the kitchen; from that measured by the peck or the bushel or the yard to that calculated by hourly rates or piece counts; work ranging from lawyering to flying jet liners, from office to assembly line, from White House to sweat shop. In short, by *work* I mean whatever people do to earn their living. No matter what the job is, its essence is unchanging: Work is the form in which we make ourselves useful to others.

Work creates civilization and culture (we will use both terms to indicate the same thing). The difference between life in the African bush and life in the Western world is *work*.

Don't African bush people work?

Yes, but at a primitive level. The bush people have to do everything for themselves. Civilization is sharing in the work of others.

It is a circle we will finally see close: Our working puts us in the service of others; the civilization that work creates puts others in the service of ourselves. Thus, work restores the broken family of humankind.

Why?

Because through work that serves others, we also serve God, and he in exchange weaves the work of others into a culture that makes our work easier and more rewarding.

As seed multiplies into a harvest under the wings of the Holy Spirit, so work multiplies into a civilization under the intricate hand of that same Spirit.

This is why work gives meaning to your life and to mine.

The Power

We know, as soon as reminded, that work spins the wheels of the world.

No work? Then nothing else either. Culture and civilization don't just happen. They are made to happen and to keep happening—by God the Holy Spirit, *through our work*.

Imagine that everyone quits working, right now! What happens? Civilized life quickly melts away. Food vanishes from the store shelves, gas pumps dry up, streets are no longer patrolled, and fires burn themselves out. Communication and transportation services end and utilities go dead. Those who survive at all are soon huddled around campfires, sleeping in tents, and clothed in rags.

The difference between barbarism and culture is, simply, work. One of the mystifying facts of history is why certain people create progressive cultures while others lag behind. Whatever that explanation, the power lies in work.

Another interesting thing is that if all workers did quit, it would not make too much difference which workers quit first—front office, boardroom, assembly line, or custodial staff. Civilized living is so closely knit that when any pieces drop out the whole fabric begins to crumple. Let city sanitation workers go out this week, and by next week streets are smothered in garbage. Give homemaking mothers leave, and many of us suddenly go hungry and see our kids running wild. Civilization is so fragile that we either all hang together or, as Ben Franklin warned during the American Revolution, "we shall all hang separately."

Incidentally, let's not make the mistake, if ever we are tempted, of estimating the importance of our work, or of any kind of work, by the public esteem it enjoys. Up-front types make news, but only workers create civilized life. The mosaic of culture, like all mosaics, derives its beauty from the contribution of each tiny bit.

The Harvest

As seeds multiply themselves into harvest, so work flowers into civilization. The second harvest parallels the first: Civilization, like the fertile fields, yields far more in return on our efforts than our particular jobs put in.

Verify that a moment by taking a casual look around the room in which you are now sitting. Just how long would it have taken you to make, piece by piece, the things you can lay eyes on?

Let's look together.

That chair you are lounging in? Could you have made it for yourself? Well, I suppose so, *if* we mean just the chair!

Perhaps you did in fact go out to buy the wood, the nails, the glue, the stuffing, the springs—and put it all together. But if by making the chair we mean assembling each part *from scratch*, that's quite another matter. How do we get, say, the wood? Go and fell a tree? But only after first making the tools for that, and putting together some kind of vehicle to haul the wood, and constructing a mill to do the lumber, and roads to drive on from place to place? In short, a lifetime or two to make one chair! We are physically unable, it is obvious, to provide ourselves from scratch with the household goods we can now see from wherever you and I are sitting—to say nothing of building and furnishing the whole house.

Consider everything else that we can use every day and never really see. Who builds and maintains the roads and streets we take for granted? Who polices them so we can move about in comparative safety? Who erects the stores, landscapes the parks, builds the freeways? Who provides the services that keep things going in good weather and bad?

Well, civilization blends work into doing all that. It's what we mean by civilization, really—goods and services to hand when we need them. There are countless workers, just like ourselves—including ourselves—whose work creates the harvest that provides each of us with far more than we could ever provide for ourselves.

Going shopping? Someone's work has already stocked the aisles with food, stuffed the racks with clothing, crowded counters with goods—for you!

Going traveling? Someone's work has already paved the highways, built the airports, designed and fueled the planes—for you!

Going abroad? Someone's work has already raised the cathedrals, painted the pictures, laid out the cities—for you!

Staying home? Someone's work enlivens TV channels, prints the daily paper, keeps social order—for you!

In trouble? Someone's work defies emergencies, defeats the storms, and has repairs ready—for you!

So everywhere and at all times, there are countless hands moving all the wheels of civilization—for you!

Work plants the seed; civilization reaps the harvest. Work is the form in which we make ourselves useful to others; civilization is the form in which others make themselves useful to us. We plant; God gives the increase to unify the human race.

Forgotten Something?

Oh, I know, you think I've forgotten something, and before you take a look around you want to be sure it's counted in.

You're thinking that what I've been saying is sentimental, as if some celestial Santa Claus dropped everything into my living room by way of the chimney. In fact, nothing is free in this old world? Pay for whatever you want, or do without it? No two ways about that!

So, then, I'm forgetting that I've *paid* for whatever it is that I own and pay my share in taxes and profits for all the public and private services I enjoy? This is what you think I've ignored? No paycheck, nothing else?

Well, no, I thought of that—and read quite a few books on economics, from old Adam Smith to Karl Marx to Kenneth Galbraith to discover just how my paycheck does relate to all those things I own and use.

Funny thing, though, these experts didn't help much.

It's too simple for the experts, probably.

As I see it now, things stand like this: Our paychecks represent our working efforts in, say, forty hours per week. Some bring in far more dollars than others, but just say that on the average each should in fact buy only what you or I could make for ourselves in the same forty hours a week. (Economics is not that simple? Maybe not, but for now let it pass—because when you start looking seriously at the meaning of civilization, my way is how you will see it, too, I think).

At least we can agree that if we both worked not only forty but, say, one hundred and forty hours a week, we ourselves couldn't make from scratch even a fraction of all the goods and services that we call our own. A funny thing happens, as they used to say, to a paycheck on its way to the bank. That paycheck turns out to buy us the use of far more than we could possibly make for ourselves in the time it takes us to earn the check. Money is the key that opens the storehouse of civilization, but a whole lot more comes flooding out through that door than we could make for ourselves in the time it takes to earn the key.

And that's true, no matter how big the check becomes.

The experts, I say, don't seem to explain that exactly.

But that's the way it is.

Goods and Services

We can profit from one useful distinction made by the experts: They talk about *goods* and *services* as the forms taken by work.

So our jobs can be divided between those that produce goods and those that render services.

Goods are things that last while services pass with the doing. The stove in your kitchen belongs to the world's goods; the cooking done on it adds to the world's services. The desk in my office is among economic goods; the work done over it joins economic services.

The reason for taking note of this distinction is to parry in advance the mistake of thinking that work invested in goods is more important than work invested in services. Goods do seem to congeal and preserve the labor invested in them, while services pass with the moment of performance.

True but misleading, because goods without attendant services do not amount to much, nor do they last very long.

A great cathedral endures, it is true, for centuries, immortalizing the hands that made it; while work spent in sweeping its floors seems to disappear with the swish of the broom. However, a building left unattended and uncared for soon serves no one but those interested in ruins. Your car unserviced, a highway unrepaired, the television set untouched, the stove left cold—such goods soon play no constructive role in civilization.

Goods and services are twins. Work invested in either knits the robe of culture. Without goods services are inept; without services goods are lame.

For Others

Our definition of work as the form in which we make ourselves useful to others is, by the way, sober economics, not some poetaster's fancy.

Goods and services are not produced as ends in themselves. Either they benefit others or there is no demand for their doing. That is to say, either they sell because they are useful to others or no one hires us to produce them.

We find work to do, in fact, only because what we do is useful, that is salable, to another.

Therefore, we can repeat that work gives meaning to life *because* work is the way in which we make ourselves useful to society.

If you still find that hard to "see," so once did I.

I found it even harder to "see" that work could even be called the "gift" of my self to the benefit of another. Before we are through, though, we just might want to insist on that—wait and see. (We will not forget to ask how this relates to the paycheck.)

Summary

All of our efforts to endow our lives with meaning are apt to come up short and disappointing. Why? Because all our passion to fill the meaning-vacuum through multiplied activity in the home, the church, the community, or whatever stumbles over that big block of every week's time we have to spend on the seeming meaninglessness of the job. The spare-time charities cannot tip the scales. Redoubling our efforts only obscures the goal.

We are sometimes advised to try giving meaning to our work (instead of finding it there) by thinking of the job in religious terms such as *calling* or *vocation*. What seems at first like a helpful perspective, however, deals with work as if from the outside. We find ourselves still trying to endow our own work with meaning. We are trying to find the content in the label, without real success. The meaning we seek has to be *in* work itself.

And so it is!

2

WORD ON WORK

The Day of Illumination

Why?

Work gives meaning to life because work is the form in which we make ourselves useful to others.

Why should this be a source of meaning?

Why does serving others give meaning to life?

We can reply that the work that places us in the service of others shares in the creation of civilization, the form in which others put themselves in our service. We get because we give—which lends meaning to giving.

This might be more than ground enough for finding meaning in working, but we can still ask: Why does God the Holy Spirit weave our work into civilization, much as he multiplies the planting of seeds into a harvest?

The answer is twofold: First, God himself chooses to be served through the work that serves others and therefore molds working into culture to provide workers with even better means of service. Second, God has so made us that through working we actually sculpt the kind of selves we each are becoming, in time and for eternity.

Both of these perspectives on the meaning of work are illumined by two familiar parables told by Jesus.

The first is commonly called the parable of the Last Judgment and the second the parable of the talents.

Judgment by Illumination

The following account of the Last Judgment reflects God's attitude toward work. The Lord says:

> "When the Son of Man comes in his glory, and all the angels with him, he will sit on his throne in heavenly glory. All the nations will be gathered before him, and he will separate the people one from another as a shepherd separates the sheep from the goats. He will put the sheep on his right and the goats on his left.
>
> "Then the King will say to those on his right, 'Come, you who are blessed by my Father; take your inheritance, the kingdom prepared for you since the creation of the world. For I was hungry and you gave me something to eat, I was thirsty and you gave me something to drink, I was a stranger and you invited me in, I needed clothes and you clothed me, I was sick and you looked after me, I was in prison and you came to visit me.'
>
> "Then the righteous will answer him, 'Lord, when did we see you hungry and feed you, or thirsty and give you something to drink? When did we see you a stranger and invite you in, or needing clothes and clothe you? When did we see you sick or in prison and go to visit you?'
>
> "The King will reply, 'I tell you the truth, whatever you did for one of the least of these brothers of mine, you did for me.'
>
> "Then he will say to those on his left, 'Depart from me, you who are cursed, into the eternal fire prepared for the devil and his angels. For I was hungry and you gave me nothing to eat, I was thirsty and you gave me nothing to drink, I was a stranger and you did not invite me in, I

needed clothes and you did not clothe me, I was sick and in prison and you did not look after me.'

"They also will answer, 'Lord, when did we see you hungry or thirsty or a stranger or needing clothes or sick or in prison, and did not help you?'

"He will reply, 'I tell you the truth, whatever you did not do for one of the least of these, you did not do for me.'

"Then they will go away to eternal punishment, but the righteous to eternal life."

—Matt. 25:31–46

Work and Judgment

The parable just quoted illumines why God the Holy Spirit weaves our work into the fabric of civilization.

I did not always read the parable that way. Once it seemed to commend special acts of giving, such as charities that we ought to be doing in our spare time.

The Lord does not specify when or where the good deeds he blesses are done, but it now seems to me that Jesus is obviously speaking of more than a vocational behavior or pastime kindnesses. Why? Because he hinges our entire eternal destiny upon giving ourselves to the service of others—and that can hardly be a pastime event. In fact, giving our selves to the service of others, as obviously required by the Lord, is precisely what the central block of life that we give to working turns out to be!

Is the Lord talking here about *work*?

Yes, I've come to think so.

Notice that the Day described in the parable might as readily be called the Day of Illumination as the Day of Judgment.

When were the sheep separated from the goats? Was it after the Lord had pronounced his judgment upon all those assembled before him? Did he, so to speak, weigh credits versus debits, pass judgment, and then proceed to separate the sheep from the goats?

11

The separation of sheep from goat is not made *after* the Lord's judgment is announced. The awful separation has taken place *before* a word is spoken: "All the nations will be gathered before him, and he will separate the people one from another as a shepherd separates the sheep from the goats. He will put the sheep on his right and the goats on his left. Then the King will say …" (Matt. 25:32–34).

First, the division; then, the explanation! Before the Lord says a word, the separation has been made. In fact, it is clear that the Judge does not make that division at all; he simply confirms it. The sheep got to the throne as already sheep; the goats got to the throne as already goats. Those who arrived as "sheep" are guided by angels to the Judge's right hand; those who arrived as "goats" are herded to his left! *Before*, mind you, a word is said! Sheep and goats are gathered with their kind *first of all*, and then what happens?

Only then, come the words of judgment.

No, not so much the words of judgment as the words of explanation! The Judge explains how those before him had qualified themselves for positioning on the right or left of his throne. Becoming sheep or goat has a history, one made by each sheep or goat for himself or herself. Each is told what he or she has spent life in becoming—and how. The parable is teaching us that we will "see" at last what day-by-day living is all about. It's a matter of becoming sheep or becoming goat. *That* is the meaning of time spent on the job and of time spent on all else.

The dividing line in all such becoming is starkly obvious: the willingness (sheep) or the refusal (goat) to give of ourselves to the service of others!

But giving self to the service of others—*that's what work is!*

"I Was ..." and You ...

I was hungry and you gave me something to eat.

The Lord is saying that where humans are hungry, there he too chooses to hunger. He waits in the hungry man or woman or child, longing to be served. Served how? By the work of those who knit the garment of civilization through the production and distribution of food!

God himself, hungering in the hungry, is served by all those who work in ...

- agriculture,
- wholesale or retail foods,
- kitchens or restaurants,
- food transportation or the mass production of food items,
- manufacturing of implements used in agriculture or in any of the countless food-related industries,
- innumerable support services and enterprises that together make food production and distribution possible.

God transforms plantings into harvests. Then he waits to be fed by those whose work turns harvests into one of the basic elements of civilization. The gift of ourselves to others through work *is* the gift of ourselves to God—and this is why work gives both temporal and eternal meaning to life!

I was thirsty and you gave me something to drink.

This parable was not composed at random. Jesus is getting at the basic necessities that civilization provides to human life—first food, now water. And God is served by those whose work contributes to the availability, distribution, and use of water—be it to slake the thirst of man, beast, or field; be it to keep the world fresh and clean and sanitary. The Lord is "thirsty" wherever water is needed and is served by all who knit the sleeve of civilization by working in ...

- · municipal or private water services,
- · purifying waters,
- · exploration for or desalinization of water,
- · well-drilling, pipe-laying, plumbing installation, or maintenance,
- · manufacturing or servicing water-related equipment,
- · working in the countless water-related goods and service industries.

The God who through the cycle of evaporation and return replenishes the earth's water supply waits on the service of those whose work refreshes the thirsty with life-giving water. The gift of ourselves to civilized life through our work *is* the gift of ourselves to God.

I needed clothes and you clothed me.

The third and last of the basic necessities that work contributes to civilization is clothing and shelter.

Jesus is indeed talking about far more than part-time and perhaps incidental charities in this parable. He is obviously talking about the civilization created by the world's work. The scope of the parable embraces all the work required to provide the physical necessities of culture.

Here Jesus is saying: I was in all who need shelter and clothing, and you are working in ...

- · textiles,
- · building and repairing of dwellings,
- · sales of clothing and shelter items,
- · fire or police or military protection of property,
- · real estate and insurance,
- · the (who knows how many) goods and service occupations related to shelter and comfort.

The Lord's choice of the kinds of services that are instanced in the parable is carefully calculated to comprehend a vast number of the jobs of humankind. The parable is about the work needed to provide the sinews of civilization. Doing such work, the Lord says, is serving his purposes in history, and in exchange he rewards workers far beyond their input with all the abundance of culture's storehouse.

"I Am ..." and You ...

You will notice a change in the caption from "I Was ..." to "I Am ..."

To stress a point!

The parable speaks in terms of time past. From the parable's point of view, it's all over. Time has been rolled up like a scroll. All the world's clocks have stopped, the bells are silent, and alarms sound no more. The trial period is ended. Life has been lived. Judge and the judged are looking back upon the irremediable. Sheep *are* sheep; goats *are* goats. Nothing left but finding that out.

Happily, for us it is not yet so!

It was not only yesterday that the Lord waited in the persons whom we can aim to serve through our work, but it is right now, today. "Now" is, in fact, all the time we ever have. We may remember the past and anticipate the future, but we live only and always in the "now," the "today." And so, the apostle cautions us, "Today, if you hear his voice, do not harden your hearts ..." (Heb. 3:15; quoting Ps. 95:7). Now is the moment to perceive that work relates us to God because it involves us in civilization. God uses our work to create and sustain culture. That, we may say again, is why work gives meaning to life!

The parable does not stop with the basic physical necessities of existence. "Man does not live on bread alone" (Deut. 8:3; quoted by Jesus in Matt. 4:4). The Lord now goes on to include other facets of culture, also created through work—so that, finally, the parable embraces all that work of any kind provides.

I was sick and you looked after me.

Human health, for example, thrives on the boundary between the physical and the mental. And the Lord says, "I was sick," and you work in …

- · medical services,
- · counseling, visiting, healing,
- · the making or selling of medicines or in related research,
- · health insurance,
- · serving others through working in any of the numerous physical or mental health-related occupations.

Psychosomatic health merges into spiritual health, a wholeness nurtured in communion with each other. To be human is to be in relation with others. Such communion is facilitated by love and communication. Indeed, communication and spiritual concern unify civilization. Culture means togetherness, a togetherness served by countless human occupations.

I was a stranger and you invited me in.

"I was a stranger," the Lord says, for all who seek communion and communication, and you work …

- · for a telephone company,
- · at delivering the mail,
- · in the church,
- · at keeping cars moving, roads open, and commercial means of travel running,
- · in the media and TV,
- · in any of the innumerable avenues of service that keep people in communication with each other and the world.

I was in prison and you came to visit me.

God chooses to be found also among social "outcasts," those whom Franz Fannon called "The Wretched of the Earth"— those literally imprisoned, the hurt (also on their jobs), and those mentally or physically held hostage by ignorance, fear, exploitation, tyranny; and you work in ...

- social services, professional or voluntary,
- law or the courts on behalf of justice,
- education,
- politics and government,
- providing employment,
- human rehabilitation,
- any of the liberating services that so many desperately need.

Including Your Own

Have we missed the particular kind of work you do?

Not surprising. There are thousands of occupations.

Recall, though, that the parable is designed to include the world's work, and the world's workers—all who do "socially useful" labor.

In this revealed light, it is clear why work not only gives meaning to life in time but to life for eternity. "To work," St. Benedict said, "is to pray!"

And we may add, "To work is to love—both God and neighbor!"

For the "love" required by the Bible is the service of God through the service of man.

And because God wills to be served through our service of others, he provides us with civilization to facilitate our working at our best.

Intention

Now a problem: If to work is to love, what then is the basis of the Lord's separation between "sheep" and "goats"?

Did only the sheep work? That is hardly likely.

1. There are those making themselves goats by working at jobs on which the Lord does *not* depend, work which sullies culture with the grime of lawlessness, selfishness, and greed—jobs that destroy rather than weave the fabric of civilization. Such work sculpts a self destined for eternal rejection.

2. We are going to observe in a moment that there is a ratio between the talents that God invests in us and how well we use them at work. This ratio plays a role in sculpting us into sheep or goat.

3. No doubt, sheep also separate from goats in the very purpose and intent for which they really work. Why do the job? For others, or for self alone? What is our aim in life? The Lord may be served by those who in fact work with self-interest only in view, who do the very least they can get away with and as poorly as the traffic will bear, taking as much and returning as little as possible—but he is served, then, as it were by accident and against the worker's intention. Surely, these become goats perhaps without knowing how or why. Sheep differs from goat, say in "set of sail" or "point of compass" or, simply, "what am I really *after*?"

4. Then there are those whose work really accomplishes so little that their paycheck is a form of welfare. They claim the fruits of civilization while investing little of themselves in return—thus staking out a claim to space on the left of the throne.

5. And, of course, there are goats who count it clever not to work—perhaps skimming off the goods of culture through clipping coupons, or making do on skid row. Goats in dinner jackets or goats in rags. "I was hungry …" and what did *you* do about it?

Perhaps the goats are surprised on that Day of Illumination because it never occurred to them that work had anything to do with the service of God! How were they to know that working—or not working—solely with their own self-interest in view was robbing God himself!

The sheep express surprise also. Was their job, nameless and insignificant as it appeared to them, *really* serving God?! And now rewarded far beyond human dreams?

Yes, just so!

Review briefly the parable again:

1. Those on the Lord's right hand put themselves there by serving the needs of others. This is what working does. What surprises them is that in so doing they were serving God himself.

2. Those on the Lord's left hand put themselves there by refusing to work as serving the needs of others, or neglecting to exploit the talents with which God endowed them. Perhaps they worked at jobs that did violence to the will of God and good of man; perhaps they never worked at all; perhaps they worked with an eye solely to self-interest, got by with whatever they could, and grabbed every key to the storehouse door that they could lay hands on by fair means or by foul. What frustrates them is the belated perception that it was God whom they were robbing in their abuse of man. It was the store of goods and services that God intended for all humankind that the goats pillaged for themselves.

The sobering import of this parable is that, in the end, both sheep and goats are simply guided to the place they have been seeking all their lives: sheep are led to the company of the Lord they served, perhaps unknowingly; goats are assigned the place where goats could alone belong—among their kind, in the alienation from each other and from God that they practiced in life. This is, by the way, the theme of Italian poet Dante's great dramatic work, *The Divine Comedy*.

We go, the great poet teaches, for eternity, exactly where we have been "aiming" to go all our lives—to the blessed union with others and with God to which we have been giving our selves, or to the alienation from God and others which we have so calculatingly practiced.

The account of that great Day of Illumination sets our work in the light of divine revelation—now!

3

WORD ON SELF

Each His Own Artist

Sculpting Selves

It becomes evident through the parable we have just been considering that work shares in the creation of more than goods and services.

Work plays a large role in the sculpting of our selves.

Recall that both sheep and goats arrived at the glorious throne without luggage—no trappings of learning, of academic degrees, of wealth, or of power. None of the scars of poverty either. Everything, much or little, has been left behind. Death strips us of all but our selves. Each comes only as sculpted into sheep or goat. How "sculpted"? Through choosing, moment by moment, for the service of others or for the sole service of self. So the parable obviously teaches. Nothing else matters any longer. All the world's distinctions are blurred out, the fame has faded, the applause no longer rings, diamonds no longer glitter, servants no longer bow and scrape, poverty no longer gnaws, failure no longer nags. The fearful no longer cringe; the proud no longer dominate. Only selves, guided to one hand or the other of the celestial Judge.

"Naked I came from my mother's womb," Job cries, "and naked I will depart"—which furnished the title for the play, "You Can't Take It with You." No, we can't! Nothing comes along but our selves—the exception which is everything!

We are apt to forget that one by-product of our working is the self we are fashioning, day by day, on the job. Indeed, that self is in fact by far the most important product we produce in the life and time granted us by divine grace.

The chisel we use to sculpt our selves is choice. It's not a chisel of our own making; it's a tool we can't avoid using. To live is to choose—even when we decline to choose, that is itself a choice. Selves are formed into sheep or goat by the "god" we serve in the choices we make in all of life. Do we choose what to think, what to say, what to do in obedience to our Creator's will? Or, do we choose in obedience to self, or to any of the many other beguiling disguises worn by the Devil? We are always in the service of some "master"—ultimately, in the service of God or of his Adversary. Obedience to God's will sculpts sheep, while rebellion molds goats. And because work looms so large in a lifetime, the choices we make on the job play a decisive role in what kind of selves we are becoming.

How do we sculpt our selves on the job? We do it with the chisel of choice, day by day. How well do we choose to do the work at hand? How well do we choose to develop and to use the talents God has given us? What is the quantity and the quality of the work we choose to turn out, every hour? How do we choose—as employer or as employee—to relate to others on the job?

Choice at work in sculpting the self is illumined by a second of our Lord's parables, which we will view from the perspective of "ratio." What is the *ratio* God expects us, by choice, to maintain between the talents that he has invested in us and the use we make of them in working? (How we use our talents elsewhere than on the job falls outside our focus here.)

Ratio

Here is a guide to sculptors—of selves! The Lord says:

> "Again, it will be like a man going on a journey, who called his servants and entrusted his property to them. To one he gave five talents of money, to another two talents, and to another one talent, each according to his ability. Then he went on his journey. The man who had received the five talents went at once and put his money to work and gained five more. So also, the one with the two talents gained two more. But the man who had received the one talent went off, dug a hole in the ground and hid his master's money.

> "After a long time the master of those servants returned and settled accounts with them. The man who had received the five talents brought the other five. 'Master,' he said, 'you entrusted me with five talents. See, I have gained five more.'

> "His master replied, 'Well done, good and faithful servant! You have been faithful with a few things; I will put you in charge of many things. Come and share your master's happiness!'

> "The man with the two talents also came. 'Master,' he said, 'you entrusted me with two talents; see, I have gained two more.'

> "His master replied, 'Well done, good and faithful servant! You have been faithful with a few things; I will put you in charge of many things. Come and share your master's happiness!'

> "Then the man who had received the one talent came. 'Master,' he said, 'I knew that you are a hard man, harvesting where you have not sown and gathering where you have not scattered seed. So I was afraid and went out and hid your talent in the ground. See, here is what belongs to you.'

> "His master replied, 'You wicked, lazy servant! So you knew that I harvest where I have not sown and gather where I have not scattered seed? Well then, you should

have put my money on deposit with the bankers, so that when I returned I would have received it back with interest.

"'Take the talent from him and give it to the one who has the ten talents. For everyone who has will be given more, and he will have an abundance. Whoever does not have, even what he has will be taken from him. And throw that worthless servant outside, into the darkness, where there will be weeping and gnashing of teeth.'"

—Matt. 24:14–30

Ratio Explained

The parable illumines the ratio that God requires between the talents he has on loan to us, and our sculpting of our selves through the use of his gifts in work that serves him.

Consider the following:

1. The Master distributes what the servants have to work with. All is on loan. So with us, God provides (a) our talents and aptitudes, and (b) the tools of civilization to facilitate our working with his gifts.

2. All initiative rests with the servants. How they employ their talents is up to them. No one to blame but themselves.

3. The master's intent is obvious: service. That is why each of the recipients of his largesse is called *servant*.

4. The servants have the initiative but can anticipate a final accounting of their stewardship. We, too, are responsible but not independent agents. God waits in final judgment—or final illumination—on the kind of self each of us sculpts through our use of his talents.

5. The faithful servant is expected to work, you noticed, at full capacity. That, then, is the ratio that God blesses—*full* use of whatever talents we are given. Five-talent people are required to turn in a five-talent performance; so also with two-talent folk, and so on. His is the choice as to our talents; ours is the duty to use them to the fullest.

6. Notice, too, that the eye of heaven sees work in its essence, and takes small account of differences among jobs that we think are very important. Five-talent people look very "successful" by all worldly standards, stirring their pride and our envy; one-talent people risk our contempt and their own despair. But in the Master's eye "ratio" levels us all. He pronounces the very same commendation on the work of the two-talented servant as he does on that of the five-talented: "Well done, good and faithful servant; you have been faithful *over a little....*" No ground for pride; no excuse for envy. What counts in the Master's sight is the ratio between gift and performance. Why? Because in that ratio lies the index to the kind of self each is sculpting.

How well am I doing what my job requires? How persistently am I reaching out to do it better? That's his concern. At issue is ratio, between gift and performance.

7. Note that each of the faithful servants received the same reward: "enter into the joy of your master." The self sculpted through work well done in the public eye, like that of famous and successful people, will receive its due reward at the Last Day. The self sculpted through work done in the most unknown of places by the most unrecognized of workers, will receive its due reward: at the Last Day. The same glorious prospect opens for both: the "joy" of the Master: "No eye has seen, no ear has heard, no mind has conceived what God has prepared for those who love him," the Apostle writes (1 Cor. 2:9).

8. It's always a matter of ratio: How well do we serve God's purposes in the world with the talents he has on loan to us?

9. And there is that third chap, the ground-digging type. Loafer? Playboy? Shrewdy? Unwilling to venture the use of his skills lest he benefit neighbor, or Master, both in his view undeserving. No intention of using his talent for the advantage of the Giver through the service of those where the Giver wills

to be found. His excuse has a familiar ring: Why should I be using my energies for anybody else? What do I owe anyone? Why let another reap what he has not planted and harvest any benefits from my efforts? Here is the goat in the making, crouched over talents deeply buried in the ground.

The end result of the "ratio" we daily establish between our talents and our work shows up all along the way in the self we are fashioning, the developing sheep or goat. In the end, the talents are recalled; the goods or services our working with them has made are left behind. Only the self we have sculpted travels on alone and exposed to that inevitable appointment with the master and his angels.

Oh yes, work gives meaning to life: It is the form in which we make ourselves useful to others, and thus to God. It shares in weaving civilization, which is the form in which others make themselves useful to us by providing us with the tools for doing our work well, and it sculpts the kind of self we are becoming through the choices we make in the handling of our talents on the job.

Talents Are for Use

The Bible takes a hard line on the loafer.

Loafers come in several varieties. Some, by inheritance, need not work—and don't! Some, by indisposition, avoid in every way doing the work they are paid for getting done. Some, by preference, panhandle. On all such loafers, and any others, God takes a grim stand.

Just as the master did on the servant who hid his talent in the ground.

God invests in us for return! For 100 percent return, as we have already observed.

"If a man will not work," St. Paul instructs, "he shall not eat" (2 Thess. 3:10).

So much for those who foolishly presume that the world owes us a living or that the love required of Christians includes supporting the scrounger. Work, if you can, or starve! God is no sentimentalist!

God does indeed display, throughout the Bible, great concern for the poor. He hears their cries, and severely condemns those who exploit them. But the poor God loves are, as is evident from St. Paul's rule requiring work in order to eat, the unwilling poor, those who are in need because they cannot find, or cannot do, work.

The Bible views refusal to work as theft: "He who has been stealing must steal no longer, but must work, doing something useful with his own hands, that he may have something to share with those in need" (Eph. 4:28).

Work is a duty.

Why?

Because God loans talents for the purpose of reaping return.

Or, to put it another way: God loans us talents to enable us to choose the kind of self we will sculpt through using them.

Summary

There is work, of course, which no society needs. The goods and services produced violate the civil or the moral codes that make civilization possible.

Such work confers no benefit upon the world and therefore gives no meaning to the life of the worker.

We need say no more about it.

Notice, too, that work can be distinguished from play.

We may expend a lot of energy in playing, but we do that for ourselves. Play is fun and relaxing, because it is always an end in itself. The desire that leads to playing is satisfied in the doing.

When playing is done for the benefit of another, such as participation in professional sports, then such play has become work.

Because work is whatever we do for another.

In a word, whatever we do for ourselves, even if we give all kinds of time and energy to it, is play.

What we do in the production of goods and services, of use to others, is work.

4

WALKING WOUNDED

To Survive the Day

Wounds

We have been looking at work—so to speak—work at large and work in general.

What about work in particular? Your job and mine?

Radio columnist Studs Terkel has authored a large volume of interviews with workers in many kinds of jobs (entitled simply *Working*, Pantheon Books, 1974), and concludes that "To survive the day is triumph enough for the walking wounded among us." Terkel is thinking of both nonprofessional and professional, of blue-collar and white-collar, of assembly line and service workers—whose interviews he molds into fascinating and instructive reading. Work, he finds, is for many people a daily wounding experience, time spent under fire.

I have had some tutors of my own on the dark side of the job. They have been adults who have turned up over a number of years to take evening speech classes that I taught for local labor unions. What a collection I might also compile of stories of blasted hopes and maimed spirits as recounted in sometimes halting tones from the speech platform. Hurt suffered to keep the job surfaced in face and gesture as the tales were told.

Terkel is not mistaken. Work can wound.

You may know many workers, and may be one of them, who find nothing wrong with their work. We've all known, or heard of, retirees who can't keep from drifting back, time and again, to where they spent their working lives, forlorn without the routine. If you are one of those who is happy on the job, rejoice in it! But keep your heart open to others not so blessed.

I judge from my listening and from reports like Terkel's, that "wounds" at work are not selective; they can afflict all types of jobs. There is as much grim frustration in the front office as there is on the line. The machine operator may worry about risking a limb while his boss frays his nerves; so the one stops off for a beer on the way home, while the other keeps dates with the shrink. It may be just as boring for executives to jet around the world on expense accounts (glamorous as they appear to most of us) as for others to be trapped by television in the living room. Probably nobody cares much more about anyone else across the swank condominium swimming pool than on the night shift. There are "wounds" enough to go around, and they come in wide variety.

For Example

Here's a brief sampling of some of the kinds of hurts I've seen through the eyes of workers responsible enough to take evening classes after a day on the job (seeking, of course, escape into a "better" one):

Call Me Nemo

Captain Nemo is a character in an adventure tale by Jules Verne, one of the early science fiction writers. Nemo commands a submarine that travels "Twenty Thousand Leagues Under the Sea" (the title of Verne's book)—written when there were no submarines!

Nemo was carefully chosen. It means "No Name."

Captain No Name! This becomes useful to the story when enemies are trying to identify the mysterious undersea ship by the custom of asking the captain's name.

Drop the "Captain" and that's about the way a lot of workers seem to feel on their jobs—just call me "Nobody"!

My work makes me anonymous. I'm a number, or a hand—and that's all that counts, my hands. Get 'em here on time, and keep 'em moving!

I'm one more tool, a machine with clothes on—as much in the front office as in the shop. And the company pays more mind to how the real tools get on than it does to me.

Galley Slave?

They used to chain galley slaves to their seats in the boats they rowed, and the overseer kept them going at full speed with a whip.

That's about the way I have to work—and don't be fooled if I happen to have an office and secretary of my own. I'm leased to the job, tied to my desk, wired to my truck cab, enslaved to my delivery route, caught in the web of professional routines, a pawn on the world economic chessboard. I'm free on weekends; in the evenings I'm too tired to care about freedom.

Who Cares?

What hurts is that no one seems to care—and I find myself not caring about anybody else either; don't want to be bothered, got troubles enough of my own.

Who cares if I'm happy or tired or lonely or worried? Nobody does!

Are my kids good or bad, well or sick? Who even wants to know if I have kids!

Nobody wants to care. Nobody wants anybody else to want him to care.

Who cares?

Do you *really* want to know?

Who Was I?

I sometimes wonder who I was when I took this job. What did I look forward to before getting trapped by the mortgage and the pension plan and seniority? What was life like before I started moving "up," as I thought, toward the top—only to be greeted by the same old treadmill, carpeted and air conditioned? Who was I then?

And who am I now? As inhuman as the mechanical monster I tend? As dull as the weekly reports I crank out? As programmed as the computers that run me?

I'm burned out, charred before my time. What's going to be left when retirement finally comes? Will I even want to retire? Or enjoy it?

Worst of All

What gets me most of all is the constant put-down. Either being ignored or belittled or griped at. Noticed only when for once I would rather not be noticed, if something goes wrong or I am behind. Come in on time for years, and then catch it for being late once.

Cripples the spirit, this knuckling under all the time. Shrinks you in on yourself, like a puckered lemon. If it were not for the paycheck, or the bonus, or the pension plan—and my debts, I might …

But I'm caught. Bend, take it, or else!

Summary

This is a sampling of hurts on the job, the kind that the "walking wounded" among the world's workers endure. Probably you could expand the list. It covers many people.

Does Christianity take any account of these woundings?

5

WORD ON WOUND

Cross-Bearing

Follow Me

Christianity long ago took full account of the wounds we may suffer at work.

"If anyone would come after me, he must deny himself and take up his cross daily and follow me" (Luke 9:23).

Is the Lord thinking of our time and, for some, hurts on the job?

There is good reason to think so; consider:

To begin with, just giving our time (no one has a limitless stock of it) to working often requires self-denial, sometimes heroic self-denial. That is, most of us have to forego much that we would rather be doing because our working requires so exhausting an investment of both time and energy. It is the grim reality of self-denial that provokes many workers to dreaming of getting out of the factory some day, or away from the office, or free from the kitchen. Only to see those dreams fade as time hastens along, as savings never do accumulate, and as age so quickly turns gray both head and hope!

Yes, the worker—each of us—knows what self-denial is. That's commonly a part of working! Isn't this exactly what the Lord requires of those who would be his followers? Self-denial for self-giving to others—that's what we do through our jobs!

"Take up your cross," the Lord adds.

Wounded workers know by experience what he means! They daily go back to shouldering the cross of unwilling spirits, of complaining muscles, of bone-weary bodies, of aching inner selves, of maimed expectations, of utter frustration—to do the jobs required of them.

What are those wounds suffered on the job, and often carried home besides, but crosses laid upon our shoulders! Indifference? Being taken for granted? No bouquets, ever? Brickbats every now and then? An endless round of drudgery? A cruel and demanding public? Obvious exploitation? No future? Mind-dulling routine? Foul-mouthed associates? Despotic boss? Dishonest employees? Sloppy performance? Customer complaints, all the worse because justified by poor workmanship in the shop? No one catches the vision? No capital?

There is no class or trade monopoly on job-related crosses. "Take up your cross …," does Jesus command? Countless workers most certainly do!

"And follow me," does he add?

Yea, Lord, we follow—to work!

Again, the Lord says: "For whoever wants to save his life will lose it, but whoever loses his life for me will save it" (Luke 9:24).

And again, obviously applicable to work.

Is it not the "sheep" who willingly surrender life on their own terms to do the job defined in terms of orders issued by others? Is it not the "goat" who twists life, when he can, to conform to his own interest, and in thus "saving" it now loses it forever?

How well workers know what surrendering life's glitter to the gloom of the workplace means!

And as the Lord God surveys his world, what a host of rugged heroes and heroines of labor he must behold! Those who rise with the sun, lifelong, to jobs that demand endless self-sacrifice, and get in return but little reward in pay and still less in recognition. Those who see no sunshine all the day long, in the caverns of the earth or the noisome dungeons of heavy industry. And those—no less heroic—who find their substantial salary and bonuses but small recompense for the burdens, and the envy, their "success" involves. Those who must day by day drive weary bodies and spent minds to one more effort. Those who wrestle with bureaucracy to keep businesses solvent long after patience and pleasure are dead. Some who exercise initiative without appreciation, but persevere well beyond the need for personal monetary reward. Mothers whose lives are poured into their families; fathers whose bodies are sacrificed that their wives and children might live. God sees migrant families struggling hopelessly from dawn to dusk; peasants who grub like slaves without hope; service employees called any time for emergencies, surrendering their family holidays or busy through the dark of night.

"Lose your life ...," is Jesus asking us? He is talking about the martyrdoms of labor too.

Job heroism has no class distinctions, only differing forms. There are frontiers all over our workaday world requiring courage and perseverance as intrepid as ever conquered any geographical frontiers. Frontiers met and bested every day, in the kitchen, in the catacombs of industry, in the glare of the front office, in the high level visibility of the rich and the powerful.

Work can be cross bearing, self-denying, and life-sacrificing; because work is following the Lord in ways of service, be that in ways hidden to all but God alone or at an envied occupation demanding sacrifices only the doer can know.

Yes, the Bible takes full account of the wounds inflicted by working. And God instructs us that in suffering, these to give our selves to the service of others, we follow the way set before his followers by the Lord Jesus himself. Christianity is not a detour around life's problems; it leads us along the narrow way of shouldering our cross and becoming "sheep" in the process!

We can, though, see our own work more realistically, too, as a means of facing the burdens it lays upon us.

Let's ask, "What's good about work—yours and mine?"

6

WORKER ON WOUND

Seeing for Ourselves

Perspective

We who work have our own share to do in setting our working in creative perspective. And above all we must constantly remind ourselves that the difference between barbarism and civilization is *work*. Our work joins us in knitting the garment of culture which we ourselves enjoy.

There are other things, such as the following:

1. The fact that work ranges far ahead of politics in bringing the peoples of the globe closer together. The multinational corporations are often the whipping boys of theorists who quietly enjoy the products while they condemn the source. And these massive conglomerates are as far from perfection as most other human inventions. But the multinationals do draw diverse sinews of labor into cooperative and constructive effort which transcends geographic boundaries, penetrates political borders, and even joins East and West, North and South, in the production of goods and services. In this way, international economic enterprise prefigures an international

political cooperation that alone is the true hope for world peace.

When politics does achieve the unifying effect of work, the world may at last enjoy a new era of peace with prosperity. The Marxists are not mistaken in the challenge: "Workers of the world unite!" They are simply mistaken in looking to Communism as the unifying force.

2. Work underlies what we commonly perceive as the highest forms of culture as well as the simplest. Trace back to their sources the noblest creations of human genius: We always come, at last, to some person or persons at work.

Great artists work! Composers work! Inventors work! Just as charismatic political leaders work! And masters of business and industrial enterprise work! Just as do countless ordinary folk like us.

3. The writer who speaks of *Leisure, the Basis of Culture* (Josef Pieper) is confused, even though he can quote some ancient Greek thinkers in his support. Work is the basis of culture. Leisure cultivated as a way of life produces no harvests but only dilettantes—drones that absorb culture without sacrificing for it, merely thieves of others' sweat.

There is one hitch to all this. We come naturally to one question: How dare I believe that my particular job really matters in a world where millions upon millions are working? We may begin a response to that natural query by thinking of the old story about why a great battle was lost. Why? Because a key general was delayed in getting to the front. Why? By his horse going lame. Why? For having cast a shoe. Why? Because nails dropped out. Why? Thanks to the blacksmith—who hammered them into the hoof carelessly. Now, who counted most in causing the defeat? Was it the general, or the smith, or the horse, or the shoe, or the nails? How would you answer that question? Could you, in fact, really answer it? Or does the story say something about the interrelated character of our world—because winning the battle needed them all, in such a way that in fact no one can be quite sure which was most important?

Just as civilization needs the work of all of us in such a way, who can tell which one of us is or is not indispensable?

True enough, in the middle of the job we sometimes want, like a child, to cry out, "Hi, Mom, watch *me!*"

And who's watching?

Let's see!

From Thread to Fabric

The fabric of civilization, like all fabrics, is made up of countless tiny threads—each thread the work of someone. Superficially, any given thread might be readily spared or replaced—that could be my job or yours. Thinking this, we go to work on the margin, so to speak, of culture: Who needs *me?*

Is this so? Is the fact that each of us might never be missed or easily be replaced proof that what we do does not matter?

Not at all!

What matters is that we *do* our work! We are daily providing the threads which join with innumerable others in making civilized life possible.

Consider once again the furniture around you. It's congealed work—and worker. Countless hands fashioned it all along the way from raw material to finished product. Our homes are furnished because there *is* a tightly woven *fabric* of civilization, or there would be no chair, no sofa, no table, and no car, no street, nothing at all. What civilizes our world is the fact that work is done. Somewhere in the whole mosaic of goods and services our work is being done too. My chair would be no more useful were it autographed by every hand that gave something to its creation! I can use it simply because everyone did their job.

Suppose that the rain drops, one after the other, opted out of a shower because, after all, what does one little droplet amount to? By itself, of course, not much. But the drops have to be in there, one by one, to make a shower; and it's the showers that make things grow. No matter that the one tiny drop is anonymous or could in theory be easily replaced. In fact, each drop combines with every other to slake the thirst of the earth.

Wholes are possible only because there are parts!

No drops—no showers. No tiny threads of work, no civilization. Doing the daily job provides the daily thread: *that* is what matters!

If we put a painting under a microscope, it becomes apparent that each color exists thanks to innumerable tiny dots. If we analyze a television screen, it is evident that the figures we see are in fact visible because each is composed of small individual units. And if we could trace our automobiles back through all the steps involved in making them, we would find workers' hands investing workers' selves every step of the way. All wholes are made up of individual parts. What matters, always, is not who can count the parts or how readily each part *could* have been replaced. What matters is that the parts are, each of them, there! What matters is that the job, each job, like yours or mine, has a doer and gets done.

Unless many workers just like ourselves did give themselves to making the chairs we are now sitting on, we would be sitting on the floor. Unless, of course, nobody ever invested himself in making us a floor. Then we would be sitting on the grass out in the backyard—unless nobody ever planted and mowed the grass! In a world without work being *done* by countless and anonymous someones, we would all be Tarzans swinging from tree to tree.

The day we went to work we locked hands with humankind in weaving the texture of civilized life—and our lives each found the key to meaning.

Our thread counts because it is *done*!

Servant of Gadgets

What about the workers (perhaps you are one of them) who are simply slaves to modern invention? Who are controlled by the latest gadgets, by the schedule, or the assembly line, or the computer—like the cuckoo on a clock? The cheery little bird may imagine that it pops out on the hour by its own choice, but we know that the cuckoo is only a slave to the mechanism ticking away below its perch. More and more workers feel that what they might call technological regress inexorably remakes man into the image of the robots it provides. Invention serves humankind, no doubt, but only by forcing more and more workers to serve it!

That's not to be denied, and you may be one of the wounded victims.

What's to be said about that kind of wounding?

Well, what would your own life, and that of the civilized world, be like if technology and its marvelous creations were abandoned? Work would slip from its civilized to its primitive forms, and we all would fall back into barbarism. How quickly life would once again fit the philosopher Hobbes' description of early man's existence, "solitary, poor, nasty, brutish, and short."

That's about our choice: technology or barbarism. Think of the chaos that threatens a city when only one system, electrical power, goes out for a few hours. It's simply far better to be one of the workers tending the needs of a huge mechanical harvester as part of some vast agribusiness than to live in a world where starvation stalks its millions of victims. Technology makes it possible to produce enough food now around the world to feed everyone—the problem has become one of honest distribution. Again, far better, isn't it, for workers to serve all the routines involved in the production of the newest drugs than to live in the era of the witch doctor? Technology has revolutionized civilization, and it promises untold achievements ahead! The work that serves it weaves the fabric of culture.

Technology wounds. No doubt about that. It may be wounding you on the job right now. It may be making you feel absolutely unnecessary, for example, or so necessary as to be running you ragged. Every day is a bruising slavery, and who can do anything about it?

Only you can, both by perceiving your work as giving meaning to your life, and by learning to "see" what constantly advancing technological progress provides, not only for others but no less for you. Thanks to technology and the machine, more persons than ever before in human history enjoy the blessings of culture. The promise of the future is unlimited, especially as work unifies the world. Those who "pay" for technological achievements by serving the robots give just that much more of themselves to cross-bearing for human progress. God is well aware of that, while his Holy Spirit uses your work to create even more miracles in cultural progress.

Many are the unsung warriors on the technological frontiers of human progress, who bear their cross and endure the wounds that the lavish gifts of modern civilization may be extended around the globe.

From Cog to Machine

Say that my wound is being just a cog in the huge industrial machine, and hardly less so in the front office than on the assembly line. And like a cog I'm robbed of all individuality, stripped of identity, a cipher.

No doubt about the validity of that complaint. Perhaps it is yours.

Again, it becomes a matter of trying to "see" things as they really are.

"Seeing," for example, that the opposite of the cog-making machine is anarchy. What if we could shatter the industrial complex to liberate the cogs, just as the home weavers tried to save their jobs by burning down the newly constructed clothing mills two hundred years ago? Would destroying modern industry liberate us? Could everyone, then, be free? No rules? No bosses? No schedules? A world freed of cogs?

Maybe, but then a world devoid of teamwork, too! No system? No cooperation? But then no industrial production! Civilization robbed of half its content. Yes, the cotton mills did once destroy the home-knitting industries—and then proceeded to clothe the world! Home industries would never have achieved that!

The more complex the economic order becomes, the more and better goods and services it will provide humankind. But the more cogs there will have to be—if the whole is to run most efficiently.

We can't have it two ways; that is, we couldn't enjoy the products of an advanced industrial system if we wanted to do as we pleased on the job. Cars don't get made that way, nor do bathtubs, nor TV sets, nor just about everything else we need to live as well as we do. Anarchy sounds fun, but it fills no storehouses with culture.

True freedom has nothing in common with doing as we please, on the job or anywhere else. Anarchy is not freedom, but license—freedom's counterfeit. When are we "free" to use the highways? When we drive as we please? No, *only* when most drivers maintain order by obeying most of the laws most of the time. Destroy the system so we drive as we please, and, of course, no one would really be free to use the road. Such "freedom" would in fact imprison most of us in our own homes to stay alive.

Freedom and order are twins, inseparable twins. On the road and on the job.

Either each of us must work according to the rules, fitting precisely into the system, or most of our effort will be wasted motion. Doing exactly the tasks assigned us is the only way to share in producing the volume and quality of goods and services that our economy is capable of creating. We are all cogs; some seem to have more "room" than others, but none can perform entirely on their own.

The utter boredom of routines and the mind-numbing monotony of endless repetition is a form of cross-bearing required of many in order that civilization may bless both them and us. For it is as true in the factory, or in the office, or anywhere, as it is on the highways—everyone is most free to draw goods and services from the storehouse of culture when everyone best meets the requirements of orderly participation in the system.

Happily, a genuine cog is a round peg in a round hole, fitted precisely to being what, at that point, the mosaic of culture requires.

There alone resides our freedom to enjoy civilized life.

7

GIVING TO RECEIVE

The Paycheck

The Bait

And now—that paycheck!

Taking comes easy.

Giving goes hard.

We are likely to *take* the goods and services that come our way from the storehouse of civilization without even considering all the work that has gone into them. We probably think only of the work that we have invested in and getting the paycheck that becomes the key to the storehouse door.

So we never view work as "giving" ourselves to the service of anyone or anything, and we would probably avoid such giving altogether were there no bait to tempt us.

That bait is the paycheck.

We "give" ourselves to our jobs because that's the only way we can earn the money to "buy into" the congealed work of others. The paycheck is the elbow that links the gift of work and the enjoyment of civilization.

That check is both carrot and stick to keep most of us punching in on time year after year. There are the few, the risk takers, out on the cutting edge of vision and progress who are drawn to their work by challenge or driven by ambition or vision without guarantee of reward. However, even they have an eye on the financial returns that work entails.

Money builds a bridge from what we want to what we can buy. Money makes much of the difference between anxiety and security, between hardship and comfort. And so money rules as an idol in many people's lives, so much an idol that St. Paul has to warn us that "the love of money is a root of all kinds of evil" (1 Tim. 6:10).

We lay hands on money via the paycheck.

The brown envelope, the piece of paper within it—these form the goal of each week's work, even after we begin to "see" that work gives meaning to life.

Work, for most of us, is the only way to money. And although the old song has it that "The Best Things in Life Are Free," almost everyone finds that money is the basic means to our "share" in the civilization that work produces. And while many theorists have proposed ways other than payment for work as the means of distributing keys to the storehouse door, no economy has created a more productive society than that which free market enterprise provides. And so for us, it's that paycheck which baits us into doing the job, like it or not, hate it or not!

Money is an unusual kind of bait, however. A mouse might ignore the cheese in the trap in hopes of dining on something else. The average worker, unlike the mouse, has very limited options: work for whatever bait the job offers ... or feel the pinch pretty soon. It's not quite "work or starve," for most of us, but it is "work or welfare." Not the happiest choice. (We will not enter, here, upon the role of unions as they affect income; important as unionization has been, it does not modify the essentials of our discussion).

We might call it compulsory baiting, these paychecks. If not "like it or lump it," it's "like it or not"—we work anyway!

To enjoy many of the gifts that the work of others provides for us in the storehouse of culture, we have to be working ourselves. We *get* because we *give*! That may not be the first economic law mentioned in textbooks, but it is a fundamental law of work-a-day life. We get the enjoyment of goods and services provided *by* others because we give ourselves to work that provides goods or services *for* others! There is a morality about working that took a long time for me to perceive: We get *because* we give! Odd, really, isn't it? The dog-eat-dog world of economics really runs on a morality it usually pretends to scorn: Why should I give? Who gives me anything? (Think again, friend!)

The paycheck is the "bait" all right—and the "bait" is the key to the storehouse door! And what a fabulous storehouse our form of civilization turns out to be! Before you bad mouth the free-market system, think on that for a while. Other storehouses look bare by comparison.

But Not a Trap

The paycheck follows upon work. Often the harder we work, the larger the paycheck—though, as many workers know, this unfortunately is not an invariable law. That is because, as we shall see, work and wage are not related as cause and effect.

Work does not give our lives meaning by way of the bait!

If the whole of our working got meaning only in the money it earns (though many there be who think so), what meaning would survive once the money was spent?

Meaning is *not* in wage or salary; however, many seek it there.

Granted, of course, we took our first job for the money we could make—no sweat, everyone does. Then we moved to another job, probably to make more money. But how easily it all could become, and for many it did become, the familiar work-to-eat and eat-to-work—that miserable treadmill with but one exit—marked "Retirement or Death"! That's the way it is for all who expect to find life's meaning in spending the money they earn—workers who therefore never seem to earn enough. That's because, of course, the meaning we crave will never be found in the accumulation of things that we buy as wildly as we like.

Of course, we do work "for" money. It's the key to enjoying the fruit of the work of others. *But* we work "at" investing ourselves in goods and services useful to others. It requires constant attention not to lose sight of the difference: *for* money, *at* giving. Work endows life with meaning because of what work *is*, not because of what it earns. Paychecks buy goods and services provided to us through the gift of selves by others, but money buys no meaning. Life's meanings are not for sale!

Work is the great equalizer—everyone has to come to it in order to find meaning in living: no short cuts, no detours, no bargain rates.

Money does oil the wheels on which the world moves, but it is human energy exercised through work that supplies the power. The lubricant is not the dynamic that makes all things go! Money does not create civilization; only work does that! Money spreads civilization around.

We need the bait, but if ever we let the bait become a trap, all the money in the world will not buy our way out.

Fair or Just

To observe what wages are, in themselves, let's ask an ancient question about the relationship between work and wages: What, in your judgment, would be a "fair" wage for your job? Or, if you are a homemaker, what might be a fair wage, if ever you got one, for all that you do?

Or, to put it another and more general way: How does the paycheck relate to your daily work?

Given our choice, most of us workers would no doubt raise our wages or salaries. Everyone would go for improved fringe benefits too.

But how would we justify our claim for more pay as "fair"? Or, if you are presently satisfied with your paycheck, what evidence do you have to show that it is, in fact, what you deserve?

Don't be surprised if you don't know; no one else does, either!

None of the experts has an answer to such questions. No one can "prove" what is a fair wage, nor, for that matter, what is a fair price or honorable profit. Across the centuries of Western history, both moralists and economists have struggled to devise a scientific scale for measuring fairness in both wage and price—with absolutely no success.

Even Karl Marx had a go at it. He was a brilliant mathematician and widely read in economic theory. Rather early in his life, Marx believed that there should be a mathematical formula for calculating exactly what any kind of work is worth. And from that we could determine, he thought, what wages ought to be.

But Marx discovered that he, like everyone before (and after) him, could not come up with the magic code that would scientifically equate work and wage. So he finally concluded that in the perfect, classless society he hoped to see established, work would be required, and rewarded, on the following basis: from each according to his ability, and to each according to his need.

This pleasingly vague formula is in fact a confession that for all his genius Karl Marx could not more precisely define a fair wage or price. Even in that best of worlds of which Marxists dream, no one will know how to measure accurately the worth of work, nor of the goods and services that work produces.

For this reason, it has become the commissar in the Communist society who determines in practice what is meant by Marx's "giving according to ability, and getting according to need." Marxism takes political form in the Communist totalitarian state under which wages and prices are set by bureaucratic and arbitrary authority. This is not, as some Marxists and liberation theologians maintain, only a passing phase in Communist development. The autocratic state is inseparable from the Communist society because wage and price will either be established in the free marketplace or by political fiat—and Communism rejects the free market. Commissars don't intend to, of course, but in fact cannot surrender the heady power a totalitarian economy both gives and requires.

However, if economic theory offers no clue to determining scientifically what is a fair wage or price, how, then, are the wages we earn and the prices we pay defined in the democratic society?

In practice, this is done in the *free* marketplace, where theoretically goods can be sold to the highest bidder, and labor power goes where wage and working conditions attract it. Successful as such economic democracy is by comparison to Communism, the system is always vulnerable to the charge of exposing the weak to exploitation by the ruthless—a matter in which the God of love and justice has a keen concern, as the Bible proclaims.

Why does the fair wage escape mathematical definition?

Because work is essentially a gift, the gift of the self to the service of others—in exchange for the paycheck. And how is a gift to be precisely evaluated? Still more because work is the gift of the worker's *self* to the service of others, and how can the value of such a gift be scientifically calculated? The "laws" of economics trip over gifts and selves. And so in talking about what wage we ought to have, and what prices we ought to pay, we need to move into another language. Not the language of science nor even of exchange but that of morality—the language of the Bible. Economics is an art, rather than a science, and subject to moral rather than mathematical norms.

The right term for evaluating gifts of selves cannot really be "fair" or "unfair" as if that could be calculated in terms of some common, objective standard. It is not a question of "fair" wage or price. We are obliged to talk, as the church long has talked, in terms of *just* or *unjust*. What is the "just" wage and price? This is the terminology of morals, not that of economic science.

The measure of what wage you or I deserve is not really economic nor calculable nor scientific.

The issue in wages (and in prices and profits) is moral, because the basic factors involved are not things but persons, not only quantity but quality, not only the production of goods and services but in these the sculpting of selves. Let's run that through again....

Conscience and the Double Track

Work and wage run, as it were, on separate, though related, tracks.

Work does not find its meaning in wage. Wage cannot be precisely related to work.

No known scientific calculation will draw the parallel tracks together.

Marxism proposes to force the two tracks into union. The result is the brutality of the totalitarian state, contaminated with the awesome inefficiency of the bureaucrat endowed with power beyond his competence.

In practice, in the democratic society, work and wage are related by the marketplace.

However, the free marketplace can easily turn into the brutal and bitter battleground that engendered Marxism in the first place. To preserve the freedom and avoid the exploitation, another factor must be involved.

That factor is morality, daughter of conscience.

This, then, is where we have come: Work is the gift of self to the service of others that becomes the fabric of civilization. Civilization is the gift of others to the service of ourselves. Wage provides the capacity to buy in on the riches of that civilization. The relationship between work and wage cannot be calculated scientifically and must be governed by the art of creative stewardship guided by moral rather than economic law.

At issue in both work and wage is always justice, both on the job and in the pay envelope—justice to employer in the work done, justice to the employee in the payment rendered. In a broader sense, justice to the employee in wage paid so that there will be market for the goods of civilization; and justice to the employer in the work done, so that the product will be salable and serviceable. The economy that would remain free must consciously choose: either this kind of justice or the ceaseless struggle between capital and labor, which is the only relationship that Marxists think possible between them.

What is a just wage? It is a paycheck that recognizes the personal relationships that underlie work and civilization. Involved are both the needs of the worker—at all levels—and success of the enterprise—in which all are involved. As we will stress in a moment, those whose work is concerned with the creation and administration of wage and price scales must be economic artists whose jobs bear heavy moral responsibility. What the traffic will bear or wage scales that only grim necessity will oblige the poor to accept are artistic guidelines that enjoy no endorsement from heaven. The search for just wage and fair price is never-ending, for the market is always changing and so are the forms required of work.

Economic justice is by no means universal even in the best of civilizations.

A migrant worker and his family may work very hard, on very long days, to bring in less than some white-collar worker may pick up in an hour.

Because there is no scientific formula for calculating the just wage, no one can "prove" that the migrant is underpaid or that the high-salaried executive gets "too much."

However, the Lord employs recession and revolution to warn that when some wages are too low and some incomes far exceed just desert, conscience is violated and God whose bounties underlie the economy is shortchanged.

The moral aspect to our daily work concerns how well the job is being done for which we are accepting our paychecks. How creatively have we developed our talents? How enthusiastically do we attack new challenges? How eagerly do we accept responsibilities? What is the "ratio" of excellence between our God-given gifts and work-produced goods and services? It is here that sheep divide from goats—both in the shop and in the board room or executive suite. The morality of the just wage corresponds to the morality of honest work—for everyone!

Work and wage move, then, on parallel tracks. There can be a close proximity between them, as when more and better work is rewarded with higher income. But neither track is the cause of the other or the goal of the other. The track representing work provides all the goods and services that together create civilized life. The track representing wage leads to the workers' own enjoyment of the fruits of the world's work.

Without the labor track, no civilization.

Without the wages track, no one to buy in, and hence nothing sold—and, again, no civilization.

Conscience relates the two tracks by way of executive stewardship, to which we turn next.

8

THE END OF THE MATTER

Executive Stewardship

Executive Stewardship

Work and wage draw together at the point where conscience functions, that is to say, work and wage tracks coalesce in persons making executive decisions.

That's what an executive is: one who makes decisions. Strictly speaking, the good executive only executes the will of others, be it management in general or the board of directors.

Stewardship?

That's the overall term for how we choose to use, moment by moment, all that God places on loan to us, for precisely the purpose of testing the sculpting power of our *executive stewardship*.

All of us, of course, are just such executives, with God's will as the mandate given us to execute.

All of us, too, are just such stewards, for we each carry about within us God's investment of life, time, and talent.

All work, we have been saying, is alike, not in form or content but in essence. Whatever work we do puts our selves into the service of others and at the same time sculpts the kind of self each is becoming. No matter what our work is.

But certain jobs unite work and wage (and price) in someone's decision. Some workers have been given talents that push them to the top, as we are likely to view it, of the economic structure. They have the awesome obligation of setting wage and price scales for employees and products. Theirs is the gift for merging all economic variables into price tags and wage rates—and their choices are as sculpting of their own selves as any others. Conscience sets before these executive stewards an ideal free-economy goal of (1) the best product; (2) produced under the best working conditions for all employees, including themselves; (3) at the best wage for everyone involved; and (4) reflecting the best efforts at every job, to be sold at the lowest price compatible with these requirements.

We have said that the twin tracks of work and wage do not meet, and cannot be scientifically related. They are bridged by morality, not by mathematics. And it is in the self-sculpting choices of wage and price scales that managers must make the twin tracks merge—under the all-seeing eye of God. It is here that justice, as defined by the will of the Creator and revealed in his Word, comes to bear upon the economy.

The executive who seeks to avoid responsibility for his choices by seeming to let the market, or what the traffic will bear, or what necessity will oblige employees to accept become his conscience is in fact putting his choices in the service of idols—and idolatry is no more acceptable to God in board rooms and executive suites than it is in the shadowed temples of paganism. Setting wages and prices, while keeping an industry or business sound and healthy, is far from easy. Failures occur. But conscience sets before managerial executives the goal of the ideal sketched above, challenging them to make their wage and price decisions with an eye fixed on justice. Such decisions sculpt selves destined for beatitude.

Executive stewardship involves us all, of course.

Have we always envied "big" names? Always wanted to be responsible for really important decisions?

Well, we are. Each of us is! Upon our decisions hangs the destiny of a human self—our own self—of more importance Jesus says than the whole world besides.

Have we always wanted to be noticed, to be watched by important people, to "play" before a really significant audience?

Well, we do. Each of us does!

We live our lives, inside and out, in the omnipresence of God! We "play" every moment before an Audience of One—who holds our destiny in his hand! Aware of that, we should live our lives as wholly unto him, every moment!

It all comes down, day by day, moment by moment to executive decision!

Ultimate Return

God is the world's primary investor. He takes the initial risk of putting life, time, and talent at the disposal of each of us.

Like all prudent investors, the Lord God is in search of return upon his capital. What "interest" does this primary investor seek on the life, time, and talent which he commits to each of us?

The final return God wants is the most precious possession any of us has—the self!

God wants the *self*—yours, mine, everyone's!

He wants each of us, then, as sheep. For only sheep spend eternity in the presence of God.

Everything comes down to this, finally: Does he get or lose you? And each of us? Sheep or goat? Do we love him first (becoming his sheep) or ourselves first (becoming goat)? What does our behavior say?

That is not only most important to God. It is, of course, of eternal importance to each of us.

All the agonies of history root in this: God leaves man free to choose between sculpting himself sheep or goat. Why does God run and oblige us to run this incalculable risk? Because a freely given love is the only kind of true love there is. God loves us freely, certainly without merit of it on our part; God chooses to risk losing us in order to receive freely our love (that is our willing obedience) in return. That is the "interest" the investing God is after.

The only immortal possession we shall ever have is ... our selves!

All else entrusted to our care, all else we could possibly assemble in the way of goods of every kind, is as nothing in comparison to what the Bible calls the "soul"—the selves we are sculpting every day!

We do a great deal of that sculpting every day on the job.

That's why working gives meaning to living!

That's the way it is, at whatever the level—by human standards—of the work we do, be it at the "top" or at the "bottom" of the ladder.

It's not, finally, on what rung of that ladder we are working.

It's all in the "love"—that is will to obey in which each of us does his job.

For that aim will determine what happens to the most precious possession entrusted to the care of each of us: the final destiny of each *self*!

Theological Note

Just one theological observation for those interested in such things: The theme of this essay is not derived from a theology of "works righteousness" nor based on the assumption that salvation can be earned by our selves. God's gifts of life, time, and talent flower in his ultimate gift: redemption in Jesus Christ to all who receive him in faith. By faith we are liberated in Christ from inherited bondage to the Devil; by faith we are restored to the spiritual liberty that enables us to draw from the Spirit strength to choose the obedience that sculpts sheep. All obedience is by faith, lived in divine grace. My thesis is simply that of St. Paul, the great apostle of faith: "work out your salvation with fear and trembling ..." (Phil. 2:12).

In short, we are indeed "saved" by faith, but faith without the works that sculpt sheep is a nonfaith; it is "dead" (James 2:26).

And Now

And now, we can say some things about work—your work, my work, and everyone's—which might have seemed strange at the beginning of our discussion.

Consider such things as the following:

1. Work is Everyman's artistry, a kind of poetry of the world, for through it is woven the delicate and balanced rhythmic structure of culture and civilization. Work is Everyman as artist. For through our work each of us not only fashions goods and services pleasing to another, but each in the same process sculpts himself, or herself, into the ultimate destiny we are really seeking. Work makes an artist's studio out of shop, kitchen, office, wherever ...

2. Work *liberates*: because work frees its product from dispersion in a miscellany of raw materials just as the artistry of the sculptor frees his statue from the cold embrace of marble.

3. Work *molds*: a wilderness into a garden, nature into a city. Human history begins in the Garden of Eden, and culminates in the New Jerusalem; man's history wends its way from one to the other on the bent backs, active minds, vivid imaginations, and straining sinews of human labor.

4. Work *mediates*: between a field and a harvest, between a harvest and human nourishment. Work unites fibers into cloth, and transforms trees into homes. Work flies the skies,

defies the darkness, explores the moon and the planets. Work is the storehouse of today's riches and tomorrow's secrets.

5. Work, said Marx, "is the language of real life." Those who escape work avoid using that language and therefore confuse merely existing with truly living.

6. Work is the mystery that provides us with far more than we could ever provide ourselves.

7. Work gives an idea a time and place. Work endows vision with reality and hope with substance.

8. Work exerts the discipline of nature upon the development of the worker's self—steel will not be treated like plastic or wood like liquid. Through work, man obeys nature's laws and thus transforms nature into his servant and himself into a work of art.

9. Work joins man with God in the development of the universe. And this leads us to a final perspective from which to "see" work—our own work—as it really is. We can put that perspective in a sentence:

Work is the form in which we make ourselves
useful to man and thus to God!

AFTERWORD

Whatever You Do:
Why Discipleship Is Withering—
And What We Can Do About It

Manifesto of The Oikonomia Network

Whatever you do, work at it with all your heart,
as working for the Lord, not for men ...
It is the Lord Christ you are serving.

—Colossians 3:23–24

Christians today urgently need to revive their commitment to whole-life discipleship. Millions of churchgoers are "Christians" for only an hour a week—Christianity is something they do on Sunday morning rather than a way of life. The withering of discipleship is one of the gravest threats facing the church today.

The main cause of the problem is that churches have disconnected discipleship from everyday life. Too often, pastors talk about our "walk with God" and "stewardship" almost exclusively in terms of formally religious activities such as worship attendance, Bible study, evangelism, and giving. As crucial as these activities are for every Christian, they will never take up more than a tiny percentage of life for those who are not in full-time ministry. The largest portion of life—our work in the home and in our jobs—is excluded from our concept of discipleship and stewardship. This leaves us preaching a faith that is not relevant to the totality of people's lives.

The Theology of Calling: Whole-Life Stewardship

In most churches today, "stewardship" only means giving and volunteering at church. However, the biblical model of stewardship encompasses our whole lives—it is primarily about who we are, not what we do—and how we cultivate the world in all our activities. Whatever you do, Paul says in Colossians 3:23-24, work at it with all your heart, because *whatever you do* you are serving the Lord Christ!

Our individual discipleship, our church communities, and our witness to society at large must recover a holistic theology of stewardship and calling. We must reintegrate our model of discipleship with the call to cultivate the world.

The central element of this perspective is that all legitimate work is a calling from God:

> *Work is a mode of human participation in God's creative and redemptive activities.*

- It manifests the image of God, exercising the regency that he gave us (Gen. 2:15) and imitating his attributes (John 5:17).
- It puts to use the talents God gives us.
- It is how we serve our neighbors in our everyday activities.
- It is one of the main ways we reflect the character of Christ (Mark 10:42–45).
- It carries out the cultural mandate—developing the potential of creation.

- It obeys God's direct command (e.g., Ex. 20:9; 2 Thess. 3:10).
- It is one of the core elements of discipleship and spiritual formation.

Work is a core element of the personal dignity of every individual; it is one of the central purposes God originally created humanity to fulfill (Gen. 2:15). Although work is often painful and difficult now, in the fallen world, work itself is not a result of the curse. It is no less beneficial or imperative than it was before the Fall—as countless biblical passages indicate (e.g., Ex. 20:9; 35:30–35; Ps. 90:17; 128:2; Prov. 12:11–14; 16:3; 18:9; 22:29; 24:27; 31:13; 31:13–31; Eccl. 3:22; 5:6; 9:10; Matt. 25:14–30; Luke 19:11–27; John 5:17; Eph. 4:28; Col. 3:23–24; 1 Thess. 4:11; 2 Thess. 3:10–12; 1 Tim. 5:8; 2 Tim. 2:6).

Reconnecting *Oikonomia* ("Stewardship") with *Oikonomia* ("Economics")

It is no coincidence that "stewardship" comes from the same Greek word (*oikonomia*) as "economics," which refers to the management of things in the world. Good stewardship *is* good management of things in the world.

Unfortunately, churches usually limit their concept of how we serve God ("stewardship") to formally religious activities. This radically separates it from our management of the creation order ("economics"). A holistic theology of *oikonomia* would re-integrate a God-centered commitment to whole-life discipleship with a God-centered commitment to cultivate the world.

Economics is usually approached in terms of mathematical data and formulae or controversial questions of public policy, but we also need to develop a theological perspective. Economics is the social system through which individuals organize and exchange their work and its fruits. All economic activity—such as owning property, buying and selling, employment, contracts, finance and investment, business and entrepreneurship—is ultimately grounded in people's work.

Just as work manifests the image of God, exercising the regency we have from him by imitating his service and care for others, economic activities manifest the image of God, exercising our regency by imitating his sovereignty, agency, providence, justice, and love. An economic order appropriate to the image of God is one that liberates people to put their talents that God gives them to use in work; it values the larger sphere of economic structures and activities that make work possible; it protects people's legitimate interest in receiving and disposing of the fruits of their own work (primarily through wages); and, it rewards individuals or holds them accountable as they serve or harm their neighbors. Such an economic order is by far the best practical way to reconcile the dignity and freedom of the individual with the needs of the community and the imperative to serve others.

"STEWARDSHIP"	"ECONOMICS"
Tiny sliver of life	*Vast majority of life*
Your calling from God	Your daily work
Serve your neighbor	Serve yourself
Generosity	Accomplishment
Spiritual	Materialistic
Church (no world)	World (no church)

"OIKONOMIA"
All of life

Work as a calling from God
Support yourself by serving others
Accomplishment empowers generosity
Spiritual and material
Church engaging the world

The Evangelical and Protestant Perspective

The sixteenth-century Reformers blasted medieval asceticism—especially its claim that church work was morally superior to other kinds of work—as both a primary cause and a primary product of legalistic self-salvation thinking. The elevation of "sacred" work as more spiritually important than "secular" work went hand in hand with the elevation of the priest as mediator between God and the layperson. When the Bible says Jesus has a direct personal saving relationship with every individual Christian, it calls every one of us to do all our work "for the Lord" and puts his claim on all of it as service to him. Therefore, the Reformers strongly insisted that the pure biblical gospel could not be separated from the affirmation of all legitimate work as equally "called" by God.

This perspective is the reason evangelical and Protestant religion has historically been distinguished from other Christian traditions by the greater priority it places on making our faith active out in world, rather than placing more priority (as other traditions do) on what goes on inside the church. But in the present day, evangelical and Protestant Christians have largely lost the perspective on stewardship and calling that originally served as the foundation of that commitment.

The Damage Being Done

It would be difficult to overstate the spiritual damage being done by the disconnect between discipleship and everyday life in most preaching. By far, most of people's waking hours are taken up not by religious activities but by work. If we offer a model of discipleship that is limited to specifically religious activities, we exclude most of life from discipleship.

In addition, the absence of a biblical perspective on stewardship and calling is facilitating the rapid growth of unbiblical perspectives that devalue and marginalize the spiritually critical sphere of work and economics. The falsehoods of the "prosperity gospel" and other forms of entitlement mentality are largely fueled by the attitude that treats work as a burden and a curse, rather than a glorious opportunity to serve God and our neighbors by participating in God's creative work through cultivation of the creation order.

More fundamentally, the widespread practice of emphasizing the crucial spiritual importance of church activities and "kingdom work" while implicitly devaluing (through silence if not through explicit denigration) other forms of work is an open invitation to a new monasticism. Much that we hear from our pulpits is already alarmingly close to the medieval outlook in which church work is treated as morally superior—implying, among many other errors, that the people who do church work are also morally superior. If we value the pure gospel, we should remember that all legitimate work done by any Christian is equally service to God and his kingdom.

The Present Need

There are several growing Christian movements that acknowledge the need to apply biblical teaching to working life. So far, they have primarily focused on bringing formally religious activities like evangelism into the workplace. We applaud these efforts and pray for their success, but we believe something more fundamental is needed. In addition to bringing religious activities into the work*place*, we must recover our lost biblical perspective on *work itself*.

Efforts to rectify our lack of a biblical perspective on economics, the social sphere of work, have been less encouraging. Some Christians, seeing the need for God's people to engage with economics, are rushing in to do so without first carefully studying Scripture and developing a well-rounded biblical perspective on this sphere. As a result, they unconsciously adopt an unbiblical and materialistic approach that conceives of human beings primarily as *consumers* whose problems can be solved by giving them money, rather than conceiving of individuals as image-bearing *producers* of value whose main economic need is for opportunities to liberate their God-given talents and apply them in service through the work to which they are called.

The Basic Ideas of Biblical "Oikonomia"

A Personal Identity Based on Whole-Life Stewardship

Every individual is made to be, in all life, God's steward over his creation household. Sin disrupts our stewardship, both internally (we are sinful) and externally (humanity's sin causes scarcity and disorder in the world). Redemption implies restoration in the stewardship role; discipleship is all life, not just religious works. Stewardship will continue to define our eternal role in the new earth.

A Personal Calling to Cultivate the Creation Order Through Work

God accomplishes his purposes (individually and socially) through our work—gifting us with abilities to cultivate creation and calling us to use them in service. The Fall made work often difficult and painful, and in worldly terms ultimately futile; it also made us sinful and self-oriented, but it did not change the underlying dynamic of the call to stewardship through work that serves others. All legitimate work is stewardship and service, so it is critical to discipleship. Although while our present work will not create the new earth, it does eternally shape the expression of God's glory.

A Personal Perspective That Sees Work and Economics Spiritually, Not Just Materially

Work and economics—including the larger structure of economic activities and institutions that facilitate work—provide indispensable meaning, purpose, and fulfillment in cultivating creation as God's stewards. We sin—in our own lives, in the economy at large, and in our approach to problems such as poverty—when we treat money and other secondary goods as though they mattered most, rather than our role as God's cultivating stewards. By restoring this role, redemption makes all our work spiritually and eternally fruitful even though it is materially and temporally futile.

A Personal Commitment to Sacrificially Support Impartial Justice and Effective Generosity

The moral laws commanding impartial justice (fair dealing and property rights) and generosity (freely giving up what we have a right to for the sake of others) are ordained to constitute and to guard the economic sphere of activity. We violate impartial justice by taking away from people (whether poor or rich) the fruits of their work without good cause; we violate generosity by neglecting to give, or by giving with legalistic motives, or by giving in ways that do more harm than good. As part of our witness and discipleship, the church and individual believers must answer the call to impartial justice and effective generosity by defending the dignity and freedom of all while sacrificially helping the poor live into their calling as stewards.

The Oikonomia Network and You

The Kern Family Foundation, in conjunction with key partners such as the Acton Institute, is building a nationwide network of seminary professors, administrators, and other interested persons who are drawn from across all disciplines and crossing boundaries of denomination and faith tradition within the broader evangelical and Protestant community. They share the view that this biblical perspective must be a part of seminary education—not as one isolated topic that students briefly study but as a key element of a holistic biblical perspective on human life—one with applications in all areas of learning and ministry. Please visit www.kffdn.org/oikonomia for more information about The Oikonomia Network or to find out if there is a role you can play.

ABOUT THE AUTHORS

LESTER DEKOSTER (1916–2009) became director of the library at Calvin College and Seminary, affiliated with the Christian Reformed Church in North America, in 1951. He earned his doctorate from the University of Michigan in 1964, after completing a dissertation on "Living Themes in the Thought of John Calvin: A Bibliographical Study." During his tenure at the college, DeKoster was influential in expanding the holdings of what would become the H. Henry Meeter Center for Calvin Studies, one of the preeminent collections of Calvinist and Reformed texts in the world. DeKoster also amassed an impressive personal library of some ten thousand books, which includes a wide array of sources testifying to both the breadth and depth of his intellectual vigor. DeKoster was a professor of speech at the college and enjoyed taking up the part of historic Christianity and confessional Reformed theology in debates on doctrinal and social issues that pressed the church throughout the following decades. Both his public debates and private correspondence were marked by a spirit of charity that tempered and directed the needed words of rebuke. After his retirement from Calvin College in 1969, DeKoster labored for a decade as the editor of *The Banner*, the denominational magazine of the Christian Reformed Church. This position provided him with another platform from which to critically engage the life of the church and the world. During this time DeKoster also launched, in collaboration with Gerard Berghoef (a longtime elder in the church) and their families, the Christian's Library Press, a publishing endeavor intended to provide timely resources both for the church's laity and its leadership.

STEPHEN J. GRABILL serves as Senior Research Scholar in Theology at the Acton Institute, a Grand Rapids, Michigan-based think tank that integrates Christian worldview with economics for leaders in the church, academy, and business sectors. He is editor emeritus of the *Journal of Markets & Morality*, as well as General Editor of the *NIV Stewardship Study Bible*, an Evangelical Christian Publishers Association (ECPA) award-contending resource, and a founding board member of Stewardship Council, the producer of the study Bible and a leader in the development and delivery of stewardship resources. Dr. Grabill graduated from Calvin Theological Seminary with a doctorate in systematic theology, after having spent more than a decade exploring the insights of the Reformed tradition on ethics, politics, and culture. He is author of *Rediscovering the Natural Law in Reformed Theological Ethics* (Eerdmans, 2006) and editor of *Sourcebook in Late-Scholastic Monetary Theory* (Lexington, 2007).

THE OIKONOMIA NETWORK is a national learning community of faculty and administrators in evangelical and Protestant seminaries who share a conviction that an integrated perspective on stewardship and economics should be a key element of seminary education. Discipleship is withering in the church today because most pastors lack this perspective, separating their concept of discipleship from the activity that defines most of our everyday life: our work, in the home and in our jobs. Founded by the Kern Family Foundation in co-operation with strategic partners, The Oikonomia Network's core principles are spelled out in the Manifesto "Whatever You Do." Network members receive financial support to conduct educational initiatives on their seminary campuses, and share ideas, feedback, resources and lessons learned with one another so that all members are building one another up. For more information or to find out if you can play a role, please go to www.kffdn.org/oikonomia.

Christian's LIBRARY PRESS

Founded in 1979 by Gerard Berghoef and Lester DeKoster, **CHRISTIAN'S LIBRARY PRESS** has been committed to publishing influential texts on church leadership, the vocation of work, and stewardship for more than thirty years. During that time Berghoef and DeKoster wrote significant works including *The Deacons Handbook*, *The Elders Handbook*, and *God's Yardstick*, which still are in demand today. After the passing of Lester DeKoster in 2009, the imprint is now administered by the Acton Institute for the Study of Religion & Liberty. For more information about Christian's Library Press, visit www.clpress.com.

ACTONINSTITUTE

With its commitment to pursue a society that is free and virtuous, the **ACTON INSTITUTE FOR THE STUDY OF RELIGION & LIBERTY** is a leading voice in the international environmental and social policy debate. With offices in Grand Rapids, Michigan, and Rome, Italy, as well as affiliates in four other nations around the world, the Acton Institute is uniquely positioned to comment on the sound economic and moral foundations necessary to sustain humane environmental and social policies. The Acton Institute is a nonprofit, ecumenical think tank working internationally to "promote a free and virtuous society characterized by individual liberty and sustained by religious principles." For more on the Acton Institute, please visit www.acton.org.